John Dunstan Breen

Anglican Orders

Are they Valid? - A Letter to a Friend

John Dunstan Breen

Anglican Orders
Are they Valid? - A Letter to a Friend

ISBN/EAN: 9783744687553

Printed in Europe, USA, Canada, Australia, Japan

Cover: Foto ©Thomas Meinert / pixelio.de

More available books at **www.hansebooks.com**

ANGLICAN ORDERS:

ARE THEY VALID?

A LETTER TO A FRIEND.

BY

J. D. BREEN, O.S.B.

"Ergo inimicus vobis factus sum, verum dicens vobis?"—*Gal.* iv. 16.

Revised and Enlarged Edition.

LEAMINGTON:
ART AND BOOK COMPANY, BEDFORD STREET.
LONDON:
BURNS AND OATES, ORCHARD ST. AND PATERNOSTER ROW
NEW YORK:
CATHOLIC PUBLICATION SOCIETY COMPANY.
1885.

STRATFORD-UPON-AVON :
PRINTED AT ST GREGORY'S PRESS.

PREFACE TO THE SECOND EDITION

THE rapid sale of this little work, and the frequent applications for fresh copies, seem to indicate that it met a want long felt, and that a second edition would be acceptable.

The author has endeavoured to make the present edition as complete a handbook of the whole question as possible. The history of Barlow has been entirely recast. It has not been thought worth while to notice the alleged recognition of Anglican Orders by the Council of Trent, and by Popes Pius IV. and Innocent XII. Canon Estcourt and others have exposed the absurdity of such a statement so completely that no one who has any reputation to lose, would now care to repeat it. This story has for some time had to be relegated to the limbo of exploded fables. The reference to the action of the Council of Trent in the first edition has also been altered, because, although true, its bearing seems to have been political rather than theological. In the hope that it may help honest and earnest souls in their search after the truth this second edition is offered to the public.

March 12th, 1885.

ANGLICAN ORDERS:

ARE THEY VALID?

●▶—◆—◀●

I HAVE received a letter from you, in which you set before me the difficulties in matters of religion that perplex you, and ask my advice in the *doubts* that harass your soul. I accept with pleasure the confidence you are pleased to repose in me, and I trust you will never have any reason to regret that you have done so. You may rest assured that my best advice is always and at all times at your service, and that any question you think fit to raise shall receive my most serious consideration.

Your communication has given me great pleasure, also, on other grounds : (1) because it shows that you are thinking, and that the grace of God is stirring within you ; and (2) because of your expressed resolve to allow no earthly consideration to hinder you from following the Divine call, and becoming an obedient child of the Church of God, when your intellect is satisfied where that Church is to be found. This resolve is worthy of you, and cannot fail to obtain the blessing it deserves, both of light and grace. At all events, it is more than sufficient to engage in your regard the sympathies of any one who has the heart of the " *Bonus animarum Pastor.*" It is not the fact that you differ from me that can ever separate us. This has arisen from accidents of birth and education, which we may regret, but over which we have had no control, and can furnish no ground of itself for not extending to you that "peace on earth towards men of *good-will*" which our Lord wished to be the inheritance of all those who truly sought Him. It is this *good-will* in you, your love of God, and your desire to do His holy Will at all costs, that unites us in spirit more than any external circumstance can part us in body; and makes me long for the day when we, who are already so joined together in heart and desire, may no longer be separated in outward communion.

This is the spirit in which I have learned from St. Augustine, that those from without are to be approached, if we would have our words receive that attention which we may think they deserve.

"Let those," he says, "treat you harshly who are not acquainted with the difficulty of attaining to truth and avoiding error. Let those treat you harshly who know not how hard it is to get rid of old prejudices. Let those treat you harshly who have not learned how very hard it is to purify the interior eye, and render it capable of contemplating the sun of the soul — truth. But as for us, we are far from this disposition towards persons who are separated from us, not by errors of their own invention, but by being entangled in those of others. We are so far from this disposition that we pray to God that, in refuting the false opinions of those whom you follow, not from malice but imprudence, He would bestow upon us that spirit of peace, which feels no other sentiment than charity, and has no other interest than that of Jesus Christ, no other wish but for your salvation." (Contra Ep. Fund., i., c. ii.)

You tell me that, as far as your information goes, you see no reason to doubt the validity of Anglican Orders, and that this is to you a point of such importance that it justifies, if it does not compel, your continuing a member of the Church of your baptism.

You have, you say, the Apostolic Succession, the

Priesthood, the Real Presence of our Lord in the Blessed Sacrament; and what more can any one desire?

I am far from agreeing with you that the question of the validity of your Orders occupies a place of such primary importance as you seem to suppose. It is, of course, true that valid orders must necessarily be found in the true Church of Christ, for they are necessary to her supernatural life, and, in fact, to her very existence; still, it does not by any means follow, that valid orders are a *note* of the true Church, and that those who possess them are necessarily within the One Fold of the One Shepherd. Nothing could be further from the truth. Any such inference is a logical fallacy.

There are, unfortunately, many men going about the world who have received the imposition of hands, whose souls have been stamped with that character of the priesthood which eternity itself is powerless to efface, and yet whose lives are a wreck, and whose office is a failure. They are unfortunate priests who, in their fall, can be compared only to Lucifer. It may be that they are apostates, it may be that they are reprobates — let them have fallen as they may, still they are priests, still they are ordered verily and indeed; and yet they may have no more claim to be considered, formally, children of the Church of God than the veriest Pagan that ever lived.

What is true of individuals is true also of religious bodies. At no period in the history of the Church have valid orders been accepted as evidence that the parties who possessed them had not suffered shipwreck concerning the faith. Most of the great heresies of the early ages were in possession of Orders of unquestionable validity ; nevertheless, in deciding whether their following were to be cut off from the communion of the Church as obstinate heretics or not, this was a point which was allowed to have no weight whatsoever.

In fact, I can at present recall very few instances of a religious body of any consequence which has revolted against the See of Peter — besides the Anglican Establishment — whose Orders have been disallowed by the Church. Your argument, therefore, " We belong to the true Church because we have valid orders," will not stand.

Not only is the possession of valid orders quite inadequate, of itself, to establish your claim to be within the fold of the Church, but it is extremely doubtful whether such an inheritance at all improves the condition of those who are in other respects *extra Ecclesiam* — whether it is not an aggravation of the guilt of schism, or, at any rate, a sort of white elephant, a gift which it is difficult to know what to do with, and which it is better to be without.

The dangers of sacrilege that encompass such persons are innumerable. There can be no doubt that to rend the seamless garment of Christ by schism or heresy is one of the deadliest sins which it is in the power of man to commit, and that those who approach the sacraments with any such stain upon their souls, trample under foot the Blood of our Lord. Now, in order that those who are entangled in schism or heresy may come to the altar with clean hands, it is necessary that their good faith be so perfect as entirely to free them from all responsibility, or complicity, not only with those who do such things, but also with those who consent to or communicate with those who do them.

This is no light matter. The number of souls is easily counted who are not, by reason of their neglect of prayer, carelessness about sin, worldliness, and religious indifference, to some extent answerable to God for being what they are.

One important consideration may here be pressed upon you. However firm you may feel yourself in your profession of what you consider the Catholic faith, you are still in Ecclesiastical communion with those who, even from your own point of view, are doing their best to turn the truth of God into a lie. You go to hear them preach, you assist at their ministrations, you receive your sacrament at their hands; in other words, you are ecclesiastically in partnership with them, and if the article of the creed, "the Communion of Saints," means anything, are morally responsible, as long as you remain so, for their denial of the faith, according to the principle laid down by St. Paul:—" Who having the justice of God, did not understand that they who do such things are worthy of death ; and not only they that do them, but *they also that consent to them that do them.*" (Rom. i. 32.) It is impossible for you to ˙say that you do not consent, constructively at least, to the denial of "the faith once delivered to the Saints," as long as you continue a member of an institution which does so, and assist it with your moral and material support.

There is, moreover, such a thing as receiving valid sacraments fruitlessly, by reason of some impediment existing in the soul, which hinders them from producing their proper effect, the grace of God. On the part of the recipient certain dispositions are required as necessary conditions to prepare the soul for the operations of Divine grace, and this preparation must commence by removing the obstacles that would hinder its working. Fire, for instance, will not melt granite, nor consume green wood, and the nullity of result is due, not to any impotence on the part of the agent, but to the unsuitable nature of the substance with which it is brought in contract. So with the soul of man. " He that *believeth* and is baptised shall be saved. He that believeth not shall be condemned." (Mark xvi. 16.)

This valid, though fruitless, reception of the sacrament may very easily occur in the case of the Blessed Sacrament. A person may approach Holy Communion in the most perfect good faith, who has confessed his sins with attrition only to a priest who has no jurisdiction whatsoever to absolve him, and whose absolution is therefore null and void. In the case of an Anglican clergyman—the question of Orders apart—the only source from which he could profess to derive his spiritual jurisdiction would be from a Bishop, who holds his jurisdiction from the Crown ; and yet he has not even a colourable pretext for claiming to act in virtue of any such commission when hearing confessions, for he would, as a rule, have to act in defiance of, rather than in obedience to, the authority of his Bishop, if he attempted to do so.

Putting aside for a moment the question of validity, all such absolutions would be invalid on the score of want of jurisdiction, and the party who in good faith might approach the altar on the strength of having received such an absolution only with attrition, would not indeed commit a formal sacrilege, but still would not receive the benefit of the Sacrament, because he has sin upon his soul, and its presence there is a bar to the entrance of the Holy Spirit under his roof. The most that we can positively assert is, that such a one has saved himself from the guilt of receiving unworthily ; for whether God will supply, by the working of his unfettered Spirit, in reward for his good will, what has not come to him through the ordinary channel, is a mystery, which can only be known on that day when the secrets of all hearts shall be revealed.

This clear conscience in dealing with holy things can only be true of those who are in the most perfect good faith, and upon whose souls has not rested any shadow of a serious doubt.

So that the fact of your having fruitful sacraments in the case of adults not in danger of death depends more on your being in the Church than having real orders.

St. Augustine (Contra Litteras Petiliani, lib. iii.,

c. 1)[1] writes thus, as to the effect which schism has in impeding the fruit of the sacraments :—"For if the baptism which Pretextatus and Felicianus have administered in the communion of Maximianus was theirs, why has it been acknowledged by you in those whom they baptised, as if it were Christ's? But if it is Christ's—as it truly is—it could be of no avail to those who had received it with the crime of schism. Of what avail do you say it could be to those whom you have received with the same baptism, except that —after the crime of their wicked separation had been blotted out by the bond of peace—they would not be obliged to receive the sacrament of holy baptism, as if they had it not ; but that, as what they possessed before was to their hurt, so now it might begin to be to their advantage ? But if this has not been furnished them in your communion—because it cannot be furnished to schismatics among schismatics—it is, however, supplied to you in the Catholic communion : not that you receive baptism as if it were wanting in you, but that that which you have received becomes fruitful. For all the sacraments of Christ are received, not to our salvation, but to our condemnation, when without the charity of the unity of Christ."

Again,[2] he says, in his discourse to the people of the Church of Cæsarea, "Outside the Catholic Church, he" [the schismatical bishop] "can have everything except salvation. He can have honour, he can have the sacrament, he can sing Alleluia, he can answer Amen, he can believe the Gospel, he can both have and preach the faith ; but nowhere, except in the Catholic Church, can he find salvation."

Again,[3] "So when any of the Donatists come over to us, we accept not their faults ; to wit, their dissention and error, which are rejected as hindrances to concord; and then we embrace them as brethren, standing with

---

[1] Gaume, iii., page 503.   [2] Gaume, ix., page 947.
[3] Gaume, ii., page 222.

them, as saith the Apostle, ' in the unity of the Spirit, in the bond of peace' (Eph. iv. 3), and acknowledge God's gifts in them, whether holy baptism, or the blessing of ordination, or the profession of continence, or the stability of virginity, or faith in the Trinity, and whatsoever others there may be ; yet, though they had all these, they were useless in the absence of charity. But who shall say that he possesses the charity of Christ, when he enters not into the unity of Christ? Thus, when any such join the Church Catholic, they do not receive what they were already in possession of : but, in order that what they formerly had may begin to be of service to them, they receive something which before was wanting to them. For in it they receive the root of charity in the bond of peace and in the society of unity, in order that those sacraments of Truth which they possess may be held unto their deliverance and not to their damnation."[1]

This, remember, was written of those who had valid orders and true faith, and whose sole offence consisted in their schismatical refusal to listen to the voice of Peter.

The Anglican cause is, on many grounds, in far greater straits than was that of the Donatists ; for, whereas the orders of the latter were admitted on all hands as valid, those of the former are as universally rejected.

The Catholic Church of the West in communion with the Holy See leads the way, and ordains absolutely—as being a layman—every Anglican bishop or cleric who submits to her authority. The Greek Church follows her example in rejecting Anglican Orders. Only lately, at the Bonn Conference, the Greek representatives, when called upon to accept such Orders as valid, utterly refused ; and Dr. Overbeck, speaking for the Orthodox Greeks in his book, " Intercommunion between the English and Orthodox

See Trelawny in Leo Orders p. 30y
Cong. ? .

---

[1] Epistola LXI. ad Theodorum Episcopum.

Churches," quotes a whole *posse* of English divines to prove that the Established Church never taught the *necessity* of Episcopal ordination; the Roman Church, he adds, is "rigorously orthodox" in ordaining *ab initio* converted Anglicans : that "the Eastern Church can but imitate her proceedings;" and that "all further controversy is broken off and indisputably settled."[1] Again, he says, "The Orthodox Church does not recognise the English Church to be a Church at all."[2]

The following is an extract from the letter of a Greek priest in possession of the writer :—" In reply to your letter of the 14th inst., I beg to state that the Orthodox Church does not recognise Anglican Orders as valid, nor is she likely to do so, nor has she made any authoritative declarations on the subject. I use your own words in the above replies, which I am sorry to have to present you only in this negative form.

"There are said to be certain Russians who are inclined to accept the affirmative of these questions, and the Abp. Lycurgus, of Syra, who had such a flattering reception in England six years ago, also inclined that way, or permitted others to think he did; but as to the former, they were too astute not to see their advantage in the step, if ever they think of taking it : and the latter is the only Bishop of our Church of late years who has (so far as I know) re-baptized an Anglican clergyman. So that the hope of the first depends upon some political gain accruing to Russia, and the hope of the latter is laid in his grave. The opinion I have heard expressed on the subject in the Patriarchal Court at Constantinople is, ' We have no means of determining this question, which the Roman Church does not also possess, and we cannot pretend that her power of judging of historical facts has been vitiated by her schism. She accepts the Orders of separated bodies who are less akin to her doctrinally than the Anglicans, and her advantage would lie in

---

[1] Page 71.   [2] Page 89.

accepting Anglican Orders if she could do so. *That she does not is the best proof that she cannot.*"

The following is an extract from a letter from the Rev. Basil E. Popove, Chaplain of the Russian Embassy, also in possession of the writer :—" The limits of a letter allow me only to state that by the law and practice of the Holy Eastern Church (Russo-Greek) an Anglican priest could only be admitted into her fold as a layman."

With both of these the Anglican Church herself is in substantial agreement. Taken not as she exists in the hopes and wishes of the best of her children, but as a whole, concrete, and actually existing corporate body, the Established Church of England has persistently repudiated the idea that she possesses Orders in our sense of the word, and is at the present moment busy in putting down those of her clergy who presume to act on any such hypothesis. So far is the necessity of Episcopal Ordination, as a divine institution, from being any part of her creed, that it was not till the passing of the Act of Uniformity in the reign of Charles II., that clergymen who officiated in the Established Church were required to have received it at all.

Those in her bosom who don the habit and office of the Catholic priest, though in her, are not of her. They can hardly conceal from themselves that they are out of humour with her whole spirit and history ; they are at issue with her authority ; and, if they would save themselves from being swamped by the full tide of public opinion and Ecclesiastical legislation which has set in so strongly against them, they will have to swim for their lives *against* the stream. Like Virgil's ship-wrecked heroes, " Apparent rari nantes in gurgite vasto."

As an instance of the teaching of Anglican autho-rities, that their clergy are not priests in our sense of the word, *i.e.*, have no power to "offer the sacrifice of the Mass and to administer the Sacrament of penance," the following extract from the charge of the Anglican

Bishop of Worcester, published June 28th, 1883, may
be quoted :—

"It is right here to call attention, in connection with
the first Prayer Book of King Edward the Sixth, to the
Ordinal or form and manner of making and consecrating of Archbishops, Bishops, Priests, and Deacons,
through the Ordinal was not printed at first as part of
the First Prayer Book but was issued separately ; for I
presume that those who wish to retain the use of the
First Prayer Book would desire the restoration of the
Ordinal also ; and there is perhaps no formulary or
document which marks more clearly the *essential
difference* between the office of ministers of the Church
of Rome, and the functions of ministers of the Church
of England.

"The words addressed by the ordaining Bishop to
candidates for the office of priest, according to the use
of Sarum, and in the Church of Rome generally, were,
' Accipe potestatem offere sacrificium Deo, missamque
celebrare tam pro vivis quam pro defunctis.' In the
Ordinal of 1549 these words were replaced by 'Take
thou authority to preach the word of God and to
minister his holy sacrament in this congregation when
thou shalt be so appointed.'

"The use of the Church of Rome prescribed what is
called ' The tradition of the instruments.' That is, the
delivery of the chalice with wine and water, and of the
paten into his hand for the candidate to touch. The
Ordinal of 1549 retaining this tradition of the instrument, adds to it the delivery of the Bible. It adds,
also, in almost the same words as we use at present, an
address to the candidates, in which their office is described as that of ' Messengers, watchmen, and stewards
of the Lord,' and which urges them ' to teach and to
premonish, to feed and provide for the Lord's family,
to seek for Christ's sheep that are dispersed abroad,
and for the children that are in the midst of this naughty
world, that they may be saved through Christ for
ever.'

" But our reformers of the 16th Century, who built up under God the Church of England, though they had thus made great progress in the second year of the reign of King Edward the Sixth did not consider the first Prayer Book and Ordinal then published perfect. There were things contained in those documents and things omitted from them which in the opinion of Churchmen of that day made revision necessary, and the Church of England in later days has ratified this judgment.

" To take the case, which I have last mentioned, of the form and manner of Ordaining of Priests. The Ordinal of 1549 retained ' the tradition of the instruments,' that is, the delivery of the cup and paten for the candidates to touch. Subsequent revision has abolished this ceremony and retained the delivery of the Bible only. And every one who is conversant with the teaching of the Church of Rome in the present day, and still more with the opinions of Roman Catholic writers of the 18th Century, is well aware that the ceremony was not abolished without reason. The ' tradition of the instruments ' was held to be an essential process in the form of ordaining priests. No ordination of a priest was valid without it. Is was then considered, and I believe that in the Church of Rome it is still considered the ordinary means of conveying the grace, which shall empower the newly ordained person to offer the sacrifice of the mass, and to administer the sacrament of penance.[1] Unless the 'tradition of the instruments' had been duly observed in his ordination no one could convert the bread and wine of Holy Communion into the very body or blood of our Lord, or effectually remit or retain the sins of penitent confessors.

" May we not say, my brethren, with confidence that it was necessary to revise the Ordinal of 1549, so as to

---

[1] This statement is inaccurate. The tradition of the Instruments is an "*integral*" part only of the present rite, and its omission would necessitate the repetition of the ceremony *sub conditione*, for reasons to be given later on.

abolish a ceremony which was supposed to give such powers? If the ceremony should now be restored to our Prayer Book, would not the retention give occasion for the wish that the effects attributed to it were restored also, and that the office and work of a priest in the Church of England are the same as what the Church of Rome believes to be committed to her ministers."

One such pronouncement, coming as it does from authority duly constituted and responsible, ought to carry more weight than all the anonymous articles ever written in a penny paper.

The *fact* that those who have busied themselves in vindicating their claim to a sacrificing priesthood have had the case decided against them by the verdict of the Christian World is one of great significance, and ought to have much weight with persons of your way of thinking. St. Augustine, in his controversy with the Donatists, was able to appeal to this fact as being quite decisive: " *Securus judicat orbis terrarum.*" The judgment of the Christian world is against you, and that settles the question.

One of the most surprising phenomena of the present Ritualistic movement is the reliance which those who lead it place on the infallibility of the conclusions of their private judgment in this matter, such a weight of external authority to the contrary notwithstanding. So much so, that they are willing to stake the salvation of their souls on the issue, that they are in the right, and all the rest of the world is in the wrong.

Individual impressions, no matter how strong, are not infallible. Between them and external realities the gulf is great indeed, and they never can suffice to raise any opinion out of the region of the probable. The testimony of such an overwhelming number of Christians must always present an insuperable barrier to certainty, and render the theology of those who are ready to send souls into eternity on the *chance* of their being true priests quite unintelligible.

It is time now to take in hand the thesis which I propose to myself to establish to your satisfaction, viz., that to avail oneself of Anglican Orders in any way must be held unlawful—for two reasons: -

I. Because historically their validity cannot be proved.

II. Because theologically they are absolutely invalid.

I.

The historical aspect of the question is necessarily a dreary one. It would be cruelty to attempt to drag an ordinary reader through the tangle in which it is involved.

I wish rather to confine your attention to the uncertainty of those facts which are necessary to the Anglican theory, so that even if I fail to satisfy you on the second point of my argument, I shall still leave you no escape from the conclusion. For the existence of a serious doubt, resulting from an hiatus in the chain of evidence, is quite as fatal to the lawfulness of exercising Anglican Orders as their absolute invalidity. In dealing with the Sacraments, it is never lawful to follow even a probable opinion in reference to a safer one—except when the salvation of a soul is at stake, and there is no other course open. For instance, it must ever be held a sacrilege to attempt to offer the Holy Sacrifice as long as there are any serious grounds for supposing that, instead of renewing the great oblation of the new law, you may only be acting a wretched parody of the most sacred mysteries of the Christian religion.

The historical events which preclude any such certainty as could render the exercise of Anglican Orders lawful are the following:—

1. The absence of any direct evidence that Barlow ever received Episcopal consecration.

William Barlow is the link that connects the present Anglican clergy with the Ancient Church. He it was

who consecrated Parker the first Protestant Archbishop
of Canterbury and the Father of the present Episcopacy; and if he should happen not to have been
consecrated himself, the whole succession derived
from him is vitiated in its source. What then are
the facts?

In reward for his services Barlow was *elected* by the
King's order Bishop of St. Asaph's early in 1536; but
before he took possession was, in April of the same
year, elected to the wealthier see of St. David's. On
the 21st of April he was in London, was confirmed
in person as Bishop of St. David's, and obtained
Cranmer's certificate of that event. On the 12th of
June following, however, in a warrant to the King-at-
Arms he is styled "*Elect* of St. David's" by Thomas
Cromwell, the King's Vicar-General, who was intimate
with Barlow, and who must have known perfectly
well whether he had been consecrated or not. Moreover, on June 30th, he took his seat in the House of
Lords, but below the Bishop of Norwich, who was
consecrated on June 11th, so that there can be no
possible doubt that up to June 12th Barlow was not
a consecrated Bishop. It is further to be noticed that
in spite of his not having been consecrated, he had on
the 26th of the previous April received the grant of
temporalities in a very ominous document, and after
that called himself and was called "Bishop of St.
David's." On April the 27th he was summoned to
the House of Peers as Bishop, and on May 1st was
enthroned at his distant see.

It remains then for us to enquire, did any consecration take place between the 12th and 30th of June?
Not only have we no evidence that such was the case,
but all the facts point quite the other way.

In Cranmer's Register there is found an entry of
Barlow's confirmation on April 21st, and a blank space
has been left in order to enter his consecration, which
remains a blank to this day. Professor Stubbs, in his
"Registrum Sacrum Anglicanum," has been able to

See page 18

supply evidence of consecration in the case of other Bishops, where the Register is missing, from Rymer and elsewhere; but for Barlow he has been able to do nothing.

In the grant of temporalities mention is made of his nomination by the King, his election by the Chapter, and his confirmation by Cranmer; but nothing is said about consecration. This omission is also ominous, as, since 1534, in consequence of Act 25 Henry VIII., cap. 20, it was usual to recite the fact of consecration in the writ. Not only is all mention of consecration omitted, but the whole tenor of the document goes to prove that no such consecration had taken place. It is quite different from the usual " restitution of the temporalities," by which the revenues of the See, which lapsed to the Crown during a vacancy, are restored to the new Bishop after his consecration, being "a grant of the custody of the temporalities on account of the *vacancy of the See*." Such grants were sometimes made to a Bishop elect before his consecration, as was done in the case of Bonner and Cranmer, but never to a consecrated Bishop. Moreover, it is not a temporary grant until his consecration, but a grant to him and his assigns " during his life." This clearly proves that the revenues of the See were assigned to Barlow for his life, not because he was the rightful and duly consecrated Bishop of the See, but because the See was vacant, and Barlow, as Bishop elect, was appointed for life the irresponsible administrator of the temporalities. Why should such a man trouble himself about consecration? He had received what was, in the eyes of the sycophants that surrounded Henry, equal to any consecration—the King's nomination, the position and emoluments of a Bishop; and what more was neccessary? He himself formulated the principle for us, thus :—" If the King's grace being Supreme Head of the Church of England, did choose, denominate and elect any layman, being learned, to

be a Bishop, that he so chosen, *without mention made* ✗
of any orders, should be as good a Bishop as he is,
or the best in England."[1]   Before all things Barlow
was the obsequious tool of the King, upon whose
favour all his advancement depended.   Now we have
it in the King's own handwriting that he claimed, in
virtue of his royal prerogative, the right not only to
appoint Bishops, but that their orders likewise were
included in his nomination and election.

Macaulay thus states the teaching of the founders
of Anglicanism at the time:—"That the King was,
under Christ, sole head of the Church, was a doctrine
which they all with one voice affirmed. . . . . . What
Henry and his favourite Councillors meant at the time
by the supremacy was certainly nothing less than the
whole power of the keys.   The King was to be the
Pope of his kingdom, the vicar of God, the expositor
of Catholic verity, the channel of sacramental grace.
He arrogated to himself the right of deciding dogma-
tically what was orthodox doctrine and what was
heresy, of drawing up and imposing confessions of
faith, and of giving religious instruction to his people.
He proclaimed that all jurisdiction, spiritual as well as
temporal, was derived from him alone, and that it was
in his power to confer Episcopal authority and to take
it away.   He actually ordered his seal to be put to
commissions, by which Bishops were appointed, who
were to exercise their functions as his deputies, and
during his pleasure.   According to this system, as
expounded by Cranmer, the King was the spiritual
as well as temporal head of the nation. . . . . . *It
was unnecessary that there should be any imposition of
hands.*   The King—such was the opinion of Cranmer
given in the plainest words—might, in virtue of authority derived from God, make a Priest; *and the Priest
so made needed no ordination whatever.*" (Hist. of
England, ch. 1.)

In fact, a bill was brought in during the following reign, and passed the third reading, authorizing the Queen to institute Bishops without any rite or ceremony. D. Ewes' *Journal of the House of Commons*, p. 52 :—" 22nd March. The bill for collating of Bishops by the Queen's Highness without rites and ceremonies, and the bill for tanners, were each of them read the third time and passed the House, and were sent up to the Lords."

There is nothing far-fetched in the supposition that Barlow was only too glad to humour the tyrant by allowing him to try his hand at making a full-blown Bishop in his own case by the royal will alone :—" A competitor for a tyrant's favour must always risk something to keep a front place ; and on this point he knew how the King was minded. Altogether he would seem to be by no means an unlikely man to have played the part assigned to him " (Cath. World, vol. xix., p. 479).

It was, moreover, an easy matter to do so. In those days the distinction between Episcopal *jurisdiction* and Episcopal *orders* was perfectly well understood, so that it was not without precedent for a man to be elected and confirmed as Bishop, to administer a See, and to defer his consecration to a convenient time. Bonner's is a case in point. He was elected and confirmed Bishop of Hereford in October, 1538, was translated to London in October, 1539, and was not consecrated till April, 1540.

On the other hand, it is urged that Barlow was in serious conflict with his Chapter, who were unwilling to yield to his exorbitant demands, and that if he had never been duly consecrated they were sure to have urged the fact against him. This contention is, however, not to the point. Barlow's legal right to administer the temporalities of the See rested not upon his *orders*, but upon his *jurisdiction ;* and besides, he was protected by the King's grant, mentioned above. To question this would have been to question the King's prerogative of Supremacy; and to do this would certainly have endangered the heads of the Canons, a risk they knew better than to expose themselves to.

It is urged further that he officiated as Bishop at the funeral of Henry VIII. without question. This, again, is not to the point. Barlow was a priest, and would not be called upon on such an occasion to perform any act that required an exercise of Episcopal orders. He had simply to say Mass. He would only have used the Pontifical insignia; but this, in a time of such confusion, may have passed without notice, because many were not acquainted with Barlow's position, and those that were, were aware that Prelates who were not Bishops, *e.g.*, Abbots, &c., might Pontificate, and that their doing so did not imply a claim to anything more than the priesthood.

At all events, it is said, Barlow assisted at the consecration of Skyp of Hereford, and Bulkley of Bangor; and how is this to be explained if he was not a consecrated Bishop? Very easily. Both these men were of the Geneva Reforming party, whose views on Orders coincided with those of Barlow, and who would submit to anything rather than offend the " Bluff King."

As a last resource the defenders of Anglican Orders appeal to the Lambeth Register, and argue that even if Barlow himself was not a Bishop, that Parker was consecrated by Hodgskyn, Suffragan of Bedford, about whose consecration there can be no doubt, as well as by Barlow, and that this would cover the defect.

The weight of authority against the validity of a consecration, where the principal consecrator is no Bishop, is so great, that even if Hodgskyn did pronounce the words of consecration as well as Barlow, as is alleged in the Lambeth Register, in no case could the Church recognize such a consecration as certainly valid. Indeed, the opposite view has practically no support whatever in theology. The fact, however, yet remains to be proved—did he do so? The following are some reasons for thinking he did not do so :—

(1.)   The Ordinal of Edward VI. prescribes that the words of consecration be said by the consecrator *alone*.

(2.)   Queen Elizabeth ordered the said Ordinal to be followed.

(3.)   Contemporary documents of unquestioned authority state explicitly that this was done. For instance, the document spoken of as a transcript of the Lambeth Register, preserved among Foxe's MSS. in the British Museum, says :—"And they did all other things prescribed by a certain book published for the consecration of Bishops by the authority of Parliament in the 5th and 6th year of Edward VI." It also speaks of Barlow as the " Consecrator," and the others as his " Assistants."

The entry in the Lambeth Register, *as it stands at present*, alters both these statements. Instead of saying that the act had been performed according to the Ordinal of Edward VI., it stated that it was performed " according to the form of a book published by authority of Parliament," and instead of representing Barlow as the *Consecrator* and the others his *Assistants*, it substitutes the names of Barlow and the others, representing them all as consecrators. This discrepancy is something for Anglicans to explain, as it clearly proves that the transcript preserved among Foxe's MSS. was not made from the entry in the Lambeth Registry as it stands at present, and that the present entry is not the original one, but a forgery of later date, made for the purpose of bolstering up a proceeding which, as it took place, was *illegal* as well as *invalid*.

The illegality of the whole affair was brought out by the law proceedings between Bonner and Horne the Protestant Bishop of Winchester. The latter tendered to Bonner the oath of Supremacy. Bonner, by the advice of counsel, challenged his right to do so, because he was not a true Bishop *such as the law required.* The judges held Bonner's plea to be good in law, and that Horne's right must be looked into. This was more than the Government cared to face. The trial was quashed and a bill brought into Parliament, supplying all defects whatever in the titles of existing Bishops, and directing that all prosecutions for refusals to take the oath of Supremacy, heretofore tendered by Bishops so consecrated, should be dropped.

In the course of these proceedings it was pointed out that the Ordinal of Edward VI. had been declared both by Parliament and Convocation in Mary's reign illegal as well as invalid, and had not been as yet legalised. Cecil was aware of this difficulty, for in a Domestic State Paper of Elizabeth, dated 1559, given by Canon Estcourt (p. 86) are found marginal notes in his handwriting pointing out the impossibility of making the affair wholly legal, as there was no Archbishop or no four Bishops, as required by a statute of Henry VIII., to be had, besides which the Ordinal of Edward VI. had not been "established by Parliament." The entry, therefore, in the Register, from which the transcript in Foxe's MSS. was made, that Parker had been consecrated according to the Ordinal of Edward VI., was a very awkward piece of evidence for Horne and his party to deal with. It was incumbent upon the Crown lawyers to devise a more convenient account of Parker's consecration for the trial, which never came off. This they did. This account is found in the Secretary's office amongst the Secretary's papers, and is the one inserted at length in the Lambeth Register. That the present entry is not the original one is clear from the fact that it agrees with the account drawn up by the Crown lawyers, which was found in the Secretary's office, and not with the transcript of the previous entry found amongst Foxe's MSS. By altering the entry, that everything had been done according to the Ordinal published by authority of Parliament in the 5th and

6th year of Edward VI., to the effect that it had been done according to the form of the book published by authority of Parliament, the legal difficulty was avoided, but a false statement is introduced into the Register. For the Ordinal of Edward VI., as well as the Sarum Ordinal, was not at the time legal, and the proceedings described in the Lambeth Register, as it exists at present, are not according to the ceremony prescribed in either rite.

The conjecture of careful students of records who have studied the book itself, seems more than probable, viz. : that a new blank book already bound was provided, and fresh entries put into it to suit existing circumstances, the original register being made away with.

The invalidity of Parker's consecration was openly challenged by the Catholic party, as may be seen in Harding's Rejoinder to Jewel's reply to him, published only five years after Parker's consecration. In answer to Harding's question if he was Bishop, Jewel answers that he was, having been consecrated by the Archbishop and other three Bishops. Harding then replies, " You were made, you say, by the consecration of the Archbishop and other three Bishops. And how, I pray, was your Archbishop himself consecrated ? What three Bishops of the realm were there to lay hands on him ? You have now uttered a worse case for yourselves than by me before named. *Your Metropolitan himself had no lawful consecration.*" Jewel has no answer to make to this. Now he was in London at the time of the Lambeth consecration, and could not have been ignorant of what had taken place. Why did he not say that Barlow consecrated Parker and was a true Bishop, whose valid consecration could not be questioned ? Why did he not appeal to the Lambeth Register and point out that, to make assurance doubly sure, Parker had had four consecrators instead of one, and that two of them had been made Bishops in Henry VIII.'s time ? What other reason can be suggested for his not doing so, except that he could not ? How explain Harding's bold attack and Jewel's silence, except on the ground that both parties knew perfectly well that Parker had been consecrated by Barlow, and that the latter had never been consecrated himself? The alteration in the present entry in the Lambeth Register, that Parker had four consecrators and not one only, as is stated in the transcript in Foxe's MSS., and prescribed by the Ordinal of Edward VI., which was undoubtedly used on the occasion, was not made without a reason. If Barlow alone was Parker's Consecrator, as was stated in Foxe's MSS., the necessity—for decency sake—of covering the fact that he was no Bishop would supply the reason why the Crown lawyers in the account they drew up represent that there were four Consecrators instead of one. The fact, however, that there must have been some good reason for inventing the extraordinary and unprecedented ceremony described in the present Lambeth Register, is strong evidence in favour of the view that Barlow was never a consecrated Bishop.

This view is further confirmed by the evidence of the old Earl of Nottingham given in Mr. Bailey's work, viz. : " Arch-bishop Parker's ordination made a great noyse about toune, that he was to be ordained such a day in Lambeth Chappel, which drew a great deal of company thither and out of curiosity I went thither myself and was present at his ordination, and *he was ordained by the form in King Edward's Common Prayer Book. I, myself (said he) had the book in my hand all the time and went along with the ordination* and when it was over I dined with em and there was an instrument drawn up of the form and order of it, which instrument I saw and read over. Some time after (I being acquainted with the Archbishop and being at Lambeth with him) he told me he had sent the instrument to Corpus Christi College in Cambridge to be laid up in their library *in perpetuam rei memoriam.*"

If this evidence is true it proves that the Ordinal of Edward VI. was used at Parker's Consecration, that

Hodgskyn was not a consecrator but only an assistant, and that the present entry in the Lambeth Register has been falsified to conceal the fact.   If not, why does it not agree with the copy in Corpus Christi College, Cambridge?   The copy in the Record office helps us to answer the question.   Certain alterations have been made in it which are found reproduced in the present clean entry in the Lambeth Register.   This proves that the document in the Record office is an older one than the present Lambeth Register, and not a copy made from it, and that the existing Register must have passed through the hands of Cecil and his lawyers before it assumed its present form.

In conclusion, one other piece of evidence may be mentioned.   The original entry copied in Foxe's MSS. gives the names of the other assistants, together with the dates of their consecration and the names of their Consecrators.   Of Barlow it says merely that he *was consecrated in the time of Henry VIII.*, but in the present entry all allusion to Barlow having been consecrated at all is suppressed.

How little the fact of a man being styled Bishop in those days proves, we see in the case of Parker. His consecration—supposing that he was consecrated —took place 17th December.   Now, we have a document, signed *per ipsam Reginam*, addressed, on the 20th of the previous October, "To the most reverend Father in Xt., Mathew, *Archbishop of Canterbury :*" and that he had the temporalities, is evident from the fact that Tunstall, who died at Lambeth, 18th November, 1559, was committed to his keeping.   He was, therefore, styled Archbishop, and had possession of his See in virtue of the Queen's election some two months before his alleged consecration.   These facts tell very strongly against the supposition that Barlow was a validly consecrated Bishop ; in fact, that he was ever anything more than a nominee of the Crown. The amount of positive evidence to the contrary is so strong, that it is quite impossible to *prove* he was anything more than this; and until this can be done, the claim of Anglicans to an unbroken Apostolic Succession must be considered in abeyance.

2. The next historical fact of importance bearing on the case is that Barlow, his associates, and successors, were heretics. They held and taught false doctrine, and on no point were they more at issue with the ancient Church of England than on the nature and office of the Christian priesthood. This I need not stay to prove, for you and all who think with you hold such men convinced of heresy.

It is only necessary to take up any High Church publication to find their modern representatives—held up to public reprobation as ignorant heretics. This is another shadow cast over the claim of Anglicans to a certainly valid priesthood. Orders conferred by heretics have, in certain cases, not been received by the Church. Though there is, I admit, a strong case in favour of their validity, there is also a strong case against them (Bingham, Antiq., iv. 7). And the existence of this strong case against them is fatal to their claim being recognized as certainly substantiated, until, at least, the Church has pronounced in their favour. Without this guarantee heretical ordinations cannot be regarded as *safe.'* You will recollect the distinction made between the orders of the Miletians and those of the Novatians and Donatists as bearing upon this point.

3. The third important fact in the list is the omission of the tradition of the instruments. This portion of the ceremony is, it is true, not primitive; still it was part of the existing rite at the time, used to render more explicit the declaration of the nature of the office conferred, and cannot be omitted without prejudice to the *status* of those so ordained. Benedict XIV.[1] mentions the case of a priest, who, *by accident*, omitted to receive the instruments from the Bishop.

---

[1] Syn. Dioc., viii. 10.

On the case being brought before the Sacred Congregation, it was decided that he must be ordained again *conditionally*. What, then, is to be said of the *intentional* omission of this part of the Ordination Service, coupled as it was with the omission of everything that had been considered of the essence of the priesthood? If the former omission was sufficient to render ordination probably invalid, the latter very much increases the probability.

4. The uncertainty as to valid baptism leaves the whole question of Ordination in inextricable confusion. The denial of baptismal regeneration has from the beginning been a tradition found in the Anglican Church. By the Gorham Judgment it has been given a legal recognition, and has been declared an opinion which any clergyman may hold and act upon. This opinion had always been acted upon by a certain number, whose lax practice rendered valid baptism almost impossible. We are all familiar with the old-fashioned cleric, who baptized with a damp finger, or who did not use water in winter, as it was too cold for the babies, or who, standing on one side of the font, sprinkled a few drops of water at sundry bundles of clothes held by several women on the other. All these practices combined to rear up generations of men who could neither confer nor receive valid orders.

Mr. Bennett, of Frome, bears witness to the fact, without apparently perceiving how deeply it affects the question of his orders. In an article on "Some Results of the Tractarian Movement," published amongst "Essays on the Church and the World,"[1] edited by Orby Shipley, he says, "Strange; yet not more strange than true, that Baptism as a Sacrament was well-nigh lost amongst the English people. Common basins were brought into the churches; while the fonts were made into flower-pots for the garden of the parsonage. It is very questionable

---

[1] Page 9, 1867.

whether water, when used, really did touch the person of the child meant to be baptized. The prayers which in the Baptismal Office asserted the doctrine of a new birth, were frequently altered in the recitation, or altogether omitted. The water was not blessed or consecrated, and the whole service was studiously mutilated to escape the doctrine which it involved."

Dr. Newman also bears witness to the fact, and estimates its bearing on the question of Orders as follows :—" Previous baptism is the condition of the valid administration of the other Sacraments. When I was in the Anglican Church I saw enough of the lax administration of baptism, even among High Church-men, though they did not, of course, intend it, to fill me with great uneasiness. Of course there are definite persons, whom one might point out, whose baptisms are sure to be valid. But my argument has nothing to do with *present* baptisms. Bishops were baptized not lately, but as children. The present Bishops were consecrated by other Bishops ; they, again, by others. What I have seen in the Anglican Church makes it very difficult for me to deny that every now and then a Bishop was a consecrator who had never been baptized. Some Bishops have been brought up in the North as Presbyterians, others as Dissenters, others as Low Churchmen, others have been baptized in the careless, perfunctory way so common ; there is, then, much reason to believe that some consecrators were not Bishops, for the simple reason that, formally speaking, they were not Christians. But, at least, there is a great presumption that, where evidently our Lord has not left a rigid rule of Baptism, He has not left a valid ordination." [1]

The consequence of this laxity may be exemplified in the case of the late Archbishop Tait. His parents were Presbyterians, and from a correspondence in the *Church Herald* and elsewhere in 1874, it was proved

---

[1] The *Month*, September, 1868, page 271.

beyond question that he never was baptized by any rite which is acknowledged as certainly valid by the better class of Anglicans. The only baptism he ever received was conferred by a Presbyterian minister named Macknight. Now, what is the value of Presbyterian baptisms, even from an Anglican point of view?

An Anglican Bishop, long resident in Scotland, speaks as follows :—

" In arriving at any conclusion regarding the nature of the administration of Baptism in the Scotch Establishment and other Presbyterian sects, it should be remembered that its ministers one and all look upon it merely as a rite—a rite which is a sign—and have no theological belief of its importance. This being so, they would naturally administer it with no particular care or exactness. And this is what I have always found. I have seen several instances of Baptism by Presbyterian ministers, of *only one* of which could I positively take upon myself to declare that it was certainly valid. *The others were all doubtful and uncertain.* Our invariable rule in dealing with converts is to baptize them *sub conditione.*" (Reunion Mag., Oct., 1877, p. 71.)

In the appendix to the " Memorials " of Mr. Hawker (p. 217), the writer expresses the same opinion in greater detail :—

" As to the validity of Presbyterian baptisms, the opinion of Dr. Jenkins, some time Master of Baliol and Dean of Wells, that they were at least doubtful, seems to be more than probable. His custom, therefore, of insisting on conditional Baptism was an excellent safeguard against error, or nullity, or invalidity of subsequent ordination. I myself, during a residence of some years in Scotland, witnessed several public baptisms of Presbyterians ; and in no case could I testify that they had been validly performed. A friend of my own (the son of a Presbyterian clergyman, but for some time a member of the Church of

England) bears me out in this experience. He was present in 1868 at St. Paul's Established Church, Glasgow, when a certain Mr. McAuslane (baptizing on behalf of the regular minister, Dr. Jamieson) used the invalid formula, 'I baptize you in the name of the Lord Jesus.' I am told that a large majority of the Scotch Episcopal clergy invariably baptize conditionally all converts from the Presbyterian communities."

It is, then, upon the chance of a Baptism proving valid, of which it is "more than probable" that it is "at the best doubtful," that the validity of Dr. Tait's subsequent ministrations as an Anglican prelate depends ; that is to say, the validity of some thousands of ordinations, and some dozen Episcopal consecrations, amongst them those of the Bishops of Bath and Wells, Exeter, Ely, Hereford, Lincoln, Oxford, Peterborough, Winchester, and St. Asaph's. Even the question of Orders apart, this uncertainty about Baptism taints the whole Anglican Succession in its source, and must go on multiplying till the end of time ; because one of the great evils of a nation being in schism from the rest of Christendom, is that should any defect in the Episcopal Succession occur, as it is a case of breeding in, there is no chance of repairing any such mishap from a purer strain.

The difficulty does not end with Tait. Archbishop Tillotson was an Anabaptist. He himself was a Puritan preacher for many years, and there is no reason to suppose that he received either Baptism or Anglican Orders as a priest.

Again, Secker, his successor, was a Dissenter, and the fact that he was ever baptized has likewise been called in question.

Three such instances as these occurring within a comparatively short period are sufficient to involve the whole question of Episcopal Succession in the Church of England in inextricable confusion and uncertainty, for the ministrations of these three so-called Archbishops as consecrators of other Bishops

must have affected nearly every Episcopal Succession
in England. How could such men be recognised as
Christian Bishops, seeing that it is doubtful if, formally
speaking, they were ever Christians at all? Or, how
could they hand on a Succession which they never
inherited?

That Baptism, as a Sacrament, was well-nigh lost
amongst the English people up to the time of the
Tractarian movement renders it quite impossible to
trace out a certainly valid Apostolic Succession.

5. It is beyond dispute that the founders of the
Anglican Church held Episcopacy to be a lawful and
praiseworthy form of Church government, but they
were very resolute against the idea that it was of
divine institution, or was able to confer grace, or was
a sacrament. This is abundantly proved both by the
words and the acts of the Reformers. Tyndale pro-
nounces on the question of the ministry as follows :—
"We choose temporal officers and read their duty to
them, and they promise to be faithful ministers, and
then are admitted. Neither is there any other manner
of ceremony at all required in making of our spiritual
officers than to choose an able person, and then to
rehearse him his duty and give him his charge, and so
put him in his room." [1]

Jewel follows in the same strain :—" How are we
to speak of the ministry of the Church, which some
have called Holy Orders? Shall we account it a
Sacrament? There is no reason to do so. It is a
heavenly office, a holy ministry or service. By such
as have this office God lighteneth our darkness. He
declareth His mind to us, He gathereth together His
scattered sheep, and publisheth to the world the glad
tidings of salvation. The Patriarchs did bear this
office. This was the office of the Prophets. . . . . No
doubt the ministering of the Gospel is highly to be

[1] "Obedience of a Christian Man," vol. i., page 259, ed.
Parker Society.

esteemed, seeing our Saviour was not ashamed to publish the will of His Father in His own person; yet it appeareth not wherever He did ordain it to be a Sacrament." [1]

On this subject Bishop Cooper's language is remarkably clear and strong. He maintains, in his "Answer to Martin Marprelate," printed in 1559, "that no form of Church government is divinely ordained; that Protestant communities, in establishing different forms, have only made a legitimate use of their Christian liberty; and that Episcopacy is peculiarly suited to England, because the English Constitution is monarchical" (Macaulay's "History of England," vol. 1, p. 77, ed. 1862).

Cranmer has not hid his light under a bushel. His answer to certain questions on the Sacraments are given by Collier (vol. ii., Appendix 49):—Q. 11. Whether a Bishop hath authority to make a priest by the Scripture or no? And whether any other but only a Bishop may make a priest? A. 'A Bishop may make a priest by the Scripture, and so can Princes and Governors also, and that by the authority of God committed to them, and the people also by election.' And in the next answer he says, 'In the New Testament he that is appointed to be a Bishop or a priest needeth no consecration, by the Scripture, for election or appointing thereto is sufficient.'"

It was only to be expected that men with such views should act up to them. Accordingly, we have an instrument by which Archbishop Grindal, Primate of All England in 1582, authorizes John Morrison, a Scotch minister, ordained by the General Synod of County Lothian of the Reformed Church of Scotland, to preach and administer the Sacraments in any part of the province of Canterbury.

In the year 1603, the Convocation (Canon 55) de-

---

[1] "A Treatise of the Sacraments," Works, vol. ii., page 1129.

clared the Church of Scotland to be a true part of the
Holy Catholic Church of Christ ; and in it there is no
Episcopal ordination or control. To meet this view,
also, the expression ordination by "imposition of
hands," was corrupted into ordination "by election"
in the Protestant Bibles of 1562, 1577, and 1579.

In fact, it was not till the passing of the Act of
Uniformity in 1662, more than a hundred years after
the Reformation began, that Episcopal ordination
was made a condition for holding office in the Established Church.

" It was by the Act of Uniformity, passed after the
Restoration, that persons not Episcopally ordained
were, for the first time, made incapable of holding
benefices.

" No man was more zealous for this law than
Clarendon, Yet he says, 'This was new: for there
had been many, and at present there were some, who
possessed benefices with cure of souls, and other
Ecclesiastical promotions, who had never received
orders but in France or Holland ; and these men
must now receive new ordination, which had always
been held unlawful in the Church, or by this Act
of Parliament be deprived of their livelihood, which
they enjoyed in the most flourishing and peaceable
time of the Church'" (Macaulay's "History of England," vol. 1, p. 79). The same author states, that
as many as two thousand such ministers resigned in
one day rather than take orders by ordination from
a Bishop.

Pius V, in his sentence against Elizabeth, condemns
her, amongst other reasons, because she had conferred
bishoprics upon persons who were not clerics (see
p. 48).

Not only, then, are Anglican Orders untrustworthy,
because for nearly three hundred years there was no
certain baptism, but also because for over a hundred
there can be no certainty about ordination.

Some time ago there was a movement for bringing

about an interchange of communion between the Anglicans and the Swedes. Dr. Pusey argued, with much force, against any such attempt, on the ground that where there was no valid priesthood there could be no true Bishops, and that the Swedish forms were insufficient to make a priest. Dr. Littledale followed him in the same line of argument. If this be true— as it most certainly is in the case of the Swedes— what becomes of the Anglicans during the period preceding the Act of Uniformity?

Here, then, are five facts of history, as hard and dry as you could wish. Any one of them is enough to cast a doubt on the validity of Anglican Orders— enough to render any attempt at using them, in a Catholic sense, unlawful. All of them taken together render it almost an impossibility that they could be valid.

It is quite a mystery to me that a man like Dr. Forbes, who must have known these things, could make such a statement as this :—" It is *absolutely certain* that Anglican Orders are valid and regular, unless the Pope's recognition be essential " (" On the Thirty-nine Articles," vol. ix., p. 717). He ought to have said rather, "unless it be quite clear that *certainly* valid Episcopal ordination, *certainly* valid priesthood, *certainly* valid baptism, true doctrine and tradition of the instruments be essential." The absence of any of these things we know to be fatal to certainly valid succession.

To assume that Barlow, because he acted as Bishop, *must* have been consecrated, and then to busy oneself about fixing the date at which his consecration *must* have taken place, is not the way in which impartial critics handle evidence upon whose correct estimation issues of grave moment depend.

II.

So far we have dealt only with the historical side of the question; we have confined ourselves to the consideration of facts, which it is impossible to deny, and of their bearing on the lawfulness of exercising Anglican Orders in view of the doubts which these facts raise as to the possibility of an unbroken succession.

Here theology comes in to our assistance; it throws fresh light on the subject, and enables us to take a step forward. Historical doubts may suffice to prove the unlawfulness of exercising Anglican Orders without closing the question of their validity. It has been by the light of theology, and not of history, that the Church has been able to decide, without hesitation, that they are not only doubtful, but absolutely invalid.

Holding her theological principles in her hand, like so many threads of Ariadne, she has been enabled to wind her way through the labyrinth of difficulties which bewilder a student who approaches the question without any such guidance.

To the consideration, therefore, of these theological principles we must now direct our attention.

A Sacrament is defined by the Book of Common Prayer to be " an outward and visible sign of an inward and spiritual grace given unto us, ordained by Christ himself, as a means whereby we receive the same, and a pledge to assure us thereof."

This definition is sufficient for our purpose, for it mentions (1), the outward visible sign ; (2), inward spiritual grace ; (3), institution by Jesus Christ ; and these are what are generally considered essential to the nature of a Sacrament.

The outward visible sign is composed of two parts ; (1), the Matter, the visible thing done or used, whose nature as a Sacrament is determined by the form ; (2), the Form, that part of the Sacrament which sanctifies the matter, so as to bestow on it the power of causing grace, and which, ordinarily at least, consists in the words pronounced by the minister.

If it is asked why any particular form of words has power to sanctify the external matter in such a way that it not only contains grace itself, but also has the power of causing grace to exist in the souls of those to whom it is applied, the only answer to such a question is, because Christ has selected them for that purpose.

In the same way, the only reason why the external visible cause, bread, produces the inward effect, life ; and why other things—wood, for instance—do not; is that God has created the former for the purpose, and the latter He has not so created.

Hence it has always been a first principle in theology, that any one who does not, either directly or indirectly, use the form instituted by Christ, or substantially alters it, cannot possibly confer the Sacrament that results from the application of the external matters which that form was ordained to bless and consecrate.

It is, moreover, necessary that the person who uses the outward and visible sign does so for the purpose of conferring the Sacrament ; else the result in the spiritual world is *nil*. For instance, it may often fall to the lot of an elderly priest to instruct the younger clergy in the manner of conferring the Sacraments, and, although the whole rite may be gone through with the utmost accuracy, no Sacrament is conferred, because what was done was not done *for the purpose* of conferring the Sacrament, but for some other.

Keeping these principles steadily in view, we are now in a position to approach the question of the validity of the Anglican rite for conferring Holy Orders.

Up to the time of the Reformation the rite for conferring Holy Orders was made up of the imposition of hands, accompanied by certain prayers, one or other of which was doubtless the form of the Sacrament. Now, the Church has not as yet decided what exact part constitutes the form ; hence the necessity for not expunging any important part is all the greater, lest in doing so we omit something essential.

" In truth, the Catholic rite, whether it differs from
itself or not in different ages, still in every age, age
after age, is itself, and nothing but itself.   It is a
concrete whole, one and indivisible, and acts *per
modum unius ;* and having been established by the
Church, and being in possession, it cannot be cut up
into bits, be docked and twisted, or split into essentials
and non-essentials, genus and species, matter and form,
at the heretical will of a Cranmer or a Ridley, or turned
into a fancy Ordinal by a Royal commission of divines,
without a sacrilege perilous to its validity " (Newman's
" Essays, Critical and Historical," vol. ii., p. 82).

If the Church ever does interfere with the rite for
conferring the Sacraments, it is chiefly by way of
addition ; she distinctly disclaims all right to make
any substantial alteration (Council of Trent, Sess. 21).

In estimating the nature of the change in the mode
of consecrating, the Reformers have saved us a great
deal of trouble by the cleanness with which they did
their work.   They were no clumsy bunglers ; but men
of decided views.   They proposed to themselves to
give practical expression to their views on Orders in
the ritual, and they did so.

The matter and form of Holy Orders are imposition
of hands and prayer ; but the question is what imposition of hands and what prayer ?   For an answer
to these questions we must consult theology.   St.
Alphonsus (l. 6, tr. 5, q. 2) gives the ordinary teaching
of theology, when he says :—" The more probable
opinion . . . . . teaches that both power of offering
sacrifice and absolving is conferred upon the priest by
the second imposition of hands alone.   It is said the
second, for, in the ordination of the priesthood, the
Bishop imposes hands three times ; first, when he
extends his hands and says nothing ; secondly, when
in company with the priests he extends his hands over
those to be ordained, and says the prayers ; thirdly,
when, after communion, he says : " *Receive the Holy
Ghost*," &c.   They (the supporters of this opinion) say,

therefore, that both power is given, not in the first
(as is certain, according to every one), nor in the
third ; for the third supposes the priests to have been
already ordained, since they have already consecrated
the Eucharist together with the Bishop ; but, in the
second, when the Bishop extends his hands together
with the priests, as is clear from the Council of Trent,
Sess. 14, c. 3, where it is said :—" *The ministers of
Extreme Unction are either Bishops, or priests rightly
ordained by them by the imposition* (observe) *of the
hands of the priesthood*, that is, which is made by the
Bishop, together with the assisting priests." He thus
concludes :—" Wherefore, *Croix No. 1245* well ob-
serves, that an ordination made without the second
imposition of hands must be repeated entirely as the
S. C. has also declared (see Bened. xiv. *de Syn.*, l. 8,
c. 10, No. 13). The reason is that he who has not
received power over the true body of Christ could not
receive it over the mystical body of Christ. But if an
Ordination be made without the third imposition of
hands, this has only to be supplied."

The prayer used in this second imposition of hands
is the one that begins, *Oremus dilectissimi*, and con-
tinues, *Exaudi nos Deus*, and must be considered
Apostolic in its origin. It is clearly referred to in the
III. Canon of the Fourth Council of Carthage, A.D. 398.
It is found in the earliest Liturgies, the Leonine, the
Gelasian, and the Gregorian, also in the Anglo-Saxon
Pontificals of Egbert and St. Dunstan, and was used
as the Form of the Sacrament of Orders up to the
days of Cranmer. So great is its importance, that in
the old Liturgies it, together with the accompanying
imposition of hands, is called the *Consecration of the
Priest*. It is to an ordination what the consecration
is to the mass, and its omission is fatal to the validity
of any ordination performed without it. This opinion
is the one that in practice must be acted upon by all
Catholic theological writers, no matter what their
views might be theoretically. For the third impo-

sition of hands in the Roman Pontifical, that after the Consecration and Communion, and also the words, " Receive the Holy Ghost, whose sins," &c., were unknown, according to Morinus and Chardon, even in the West for 1,200 years, and then introduced only to emphasise the bestowal of judicial power *in foro interiore* over the mystical body of Christ upon one who had already received the full power of the priesthood over the real body of Christ. In the Ordinal of Edward VI., the second imposition of hands and the prayer of consecration, *i.e.*, the real matter and form of the Sacrament, were omitted bodily. The third imposition of hands alone was retained, together with the following words : — " Receive the Holy Ghost ; whose sins thou dost forgive, they are forgiven ; and whose sins thou dost retain, they are retained. And be thou a faithful Dispenser of the Word of God and of His holy Sacraments : in the name of the Father and of the Son and of the Holy Ghost." This form was a compromise between Catholicity and Calvinism. The latter portion was the invention of Cranmer himself, and the first was also of comparatively recent introduction in the Ritual, so that for the purpose of making a real priest it was worthless. This positively settles the question, for where there is no valid priesthood there can be no real Episcopate. There can be no question of consecration *per saltum* in the case of a Bishop. The priesthood is as essential as Baptism to a valid Episcopal Consecration ; one reason is, that it is by no means certain that the Episcopate is a distinct order from the priesthood, and differs from it in kind as well as ·in degree, so that one who has not the Sacerdotium cannot have the Summum Sacerdotium.

As if to remove all excuse from future generations of Anglicans for claiming an unbroken Episcopal Succession, Cranmer laid his hands also upon the rite for the Consecration of Bishops. As far back as the Council of Carthage, referred to above, the consecration of a Bishop is described as follows :—" When a Bishop is ordained, let two Bishops place and hold the copy of the Gospels over his head and neck ; and while one is saying over him the *Benediction*, let all the other Bishops touch his head with their hands." (Can. ii.) This *Benediction*, given in all the old Liturgies of the West, begins, " *Deus honorum omnium*," together with its introduction, " *Propitiare Domine*," and is styled, to mark its importance—*the Consecration*. This imposition of hands and this prayer are the matter and form of Episcopal Orders.

The words, " Receive the Holy Ghost," &c., cannot be the sacramental form of Episcopal Consecration. They are unknown in the Greek and Syriac rites, and not only so, but are of recent introduction in the West. " They do not occur," says Chardon, writing in 1745, " in Latin Rituals which are older than 400 years, and they are wanting even in several modern ones " (tom v. De l'ordre, ch. 1).

Morinus and Martene testify substantially the same thing. " None of the English Pontificals except the Exeter contain this form " (Maskell Monument. Rit., vol. ii., p. 274). When Archbishop Chichele was consecrated by Pope Gregory XII. at Siena, in 1408, the fact that these words were used was considered so remarkable, that it was recorded in the Register of the event.

In the Anglican Ritual devised by Cranmer in the reign of Edward VI., the following equivocal and meagre exhortation was substituted for the form in the Pontifical :—" Take the Holy Ghost ; and remember thou stir up the grace of God which is in thee by the imposition of hands ; for God hath not given us the spirit of fear, but of power and love and soberness."

These words are accompanied by imposition of hands, and hence the only ones that can claim to be the Form of the Sacrament. They are quite ambiguous ; they do not determine the action any way, for they mention neither the order to be conferred nor the special end for which the words are used.

They are, moreover, of recent origin. The latter portion is an innovation of Cranmer; the former, "Take the Holy Ghost," &c., used in the third imposition of hands in the old Ritual, was, however, not introduced into it till about the fourteenth century, as Martine has proved ("De Antiquis Ecclesiæ Ritibus").[1]

The whole of the part of the rite by which, and by which alone, orders had been conferred in the West for the first fourteen centuries was swept clean away ; all that was left was an addition, made to render the rite more explicit, and claiming no higher antiquity than the 14th century. Whatever part of the Ritual, therefore, may claim to be the form instituted by Jesus Christ for giving the grace of Orders, this clearly cannot put forward any such claim. For, in order to take up such a position, it would be necessary to adopt the suicidal defence, either that the form of the Sacrament has been altered, which would mean that the Sacrament had been destroyed—for the matter and form have always been considered of the essence of the Sacrament—or that the ancient Church had no true priesthood or legitimate ministers. Courayer, whom Anglican writers have championed so lustily, sees the force of this argument so plainly that he maintains that the words, "Receive the Holy Ghost," cannot be the form of the Sacrament, for reasons which he takes from Morinus.[2]

It is curious that he and his following do not see that thereby they cut from under their feet the only defence on which the validity of Anglican orders could stand.

Dr. Lingard also perceives this difficulty, and sees no alternative but to accept the monition tacked on to the words, "Take the Holy Ghost," as the only portion of the service that could be regarded as a substitute for the " Prayer of Consecration " in the

---

[1] Lib. I., art. x., n. 14.   [2] " Dissertation," page 11.

old Rituals, which was generally considered to contain the essential Form of Holy Orders. He deals with the question as follows :—

" However, setting Barlow aside, there still remained the very important question, whether the Lambeth rite was of itself sufficient to constitute a Christian Bishop; for the reader is not to suppose that the consecration of Dr. Parker was celebrated according to the form in which Episcopal consecrations are performed at the present time. In Edward's reign Archbishop Cranmer had ' devised ' an Ordinal, in conformity with his own Calvinistic notions respecting the Episcopal character. It seems, however, not to have harmonized perfectly with the notions which Barlow and his coadjutors had acquired from their foreign masters. Omitting, therefore, part of it, they consecrated the new Archbishop in the following manner. Placing their hands upon his head, they admonished him thus :—' Remember that thou stir up the grace of God which is in thee by imposition of hands, for God hath not given us the spirit of fear, but of power and love and of soberness.' How, it was asked, could this monition make a Bishop? It bore no immediate connection with the Episcopal character. It designated none of the peculiar duties incumbent on a Bishop. It was as fit a form for the ordination of a parish clerk as for the spiritual ruler of a diocese. Parliament, in the eighth of Elizabeth, ordered that the Ordinal devised under Edward VI. should be observed, which Ordinal continued in force till the Convocation in 1662 made the following alteration in the form to be henceforth observed :—' Receive the Holy Ghost, *for the office and work of a Bishop in the Church of God, committed unto thee by the imposition of our hands in the name of the Father and of the Son and of the Holy Ghost;* and remember that thou stir up the grace of God which *is given to thee by this imposition of our hands;* for God hath not given us the spirit of fear, but of power and love and soberness.' This addition was

manifestly a great improvement, inasmuch as it im-
parted to the rite that Episcopal character which it
had hitherto wanted; but, to have been of any real
use, it ought to have been introduced at the same
time with the line of prelates to whom it applied. By
Charles II. it was approved, and at his recommenda-
tion was established by Parliament as the legal form
of ordaining Bishops in the Church of England"
("History of England," vol. vi., Note C).

We must also bear in mind that the new Anglican
Ritual was drawn up to suit the new doctrine, which
was a direct contradiction of the teaching of the
old Church of England on the nature of the Sacrament.

As an evidence that Cranmer and his party did not
intend to do away with the old priesthood, stress is
sometimes laid upon the fact that the term *priest* is
retained in their Ordinal. A term, however, is worth
only as much as it means in the mouths of those who
use it. They dared not reject the term altogether,
but they took very good care to take the sting out of
it by making it identical with the Protestant term
minister, which meant one not necessarily more than
a lay officer. The Litany spoke of "Bishops, Pastors,
and *Ministers* of the Church," evidently including
officials not in orders. For instance, in the Communion
Service, the celebrant is described as a *minister* when
he received and gave Communion, and in the Marriage
Service the term "priest" is used eight times, and
"minister" thirteen times, to describe the same person. Not only so, but the word "altar," a necessary
correlative of any real priesthood, was carefully
excluded from the Prayer Book and Ordinal; the
word "table" being substituted for it, and the altars
themselves pulled down. Grindal in York, A.D. 1571
(Wilkins iv., 269), directs, "All altars to be pulled
down to the ground, and the altar stones defaced and
bestowed to some common use." Small evidence
here of any intention to retain the old priesthood.

Our forefathers had been simple enough to believe that Orders was a Sacrament, which, like all Sacraments, conferred grace, as a superadded and abiding quality on the soul, and impressed a *character* which constituted the priesthood. The new teachers changed all this, and held that Orders was not a Sacrament; that it was only an appointment to an office; that the mode of appointment was not a divine institution, and had no promise of grace attached to it; that they were, in fact, ministers, whose chief office was that of public speaking and public reading.

Here, then, we have to deal, not simply with an accidental omission, nor with an omission which had no doctrinal significance in the eyes of those who were responsible for it, but with a change made by those who had no right to make it, and made for the purpose of putting an end for ever to all claim to the inheritance of Orders as a sacramental grace on the part of those so ordained. The teaching of the 25th Article is quite clear on the point, where it says that Orders is one of those things " not to be counted for Sacraments of the Gospel, being such as have grown partly of the corrupt following of the Apostles, partly are states of life allowed in the Scriptures; but yet have not the like nature of Sacraments with Baptism and the Lord's Supper, for that they have not any visible sign or ceremony ordained of God."

Hence, even if what was said or done might otherwise have been in itself sufficient, the fact that the words used were not used as a sacramental form, and that the alteration made in them was made with a view of excluding all question of grace, and of preventing their being considered any part of a sacramental sign, is sufficient to hinder any bestowal of grace.

It is not said, or even implied, that a man who holds an heretical opinion on the nature of a Sacrament may not confer it validly, provided the form and intention of the Church have not been interfered with. When, however, as in this case, the heretical view annihilates the very essence of the Sacrament, and is given external expression by corrupting the essential prayers or ceremonies, it must be held to vitiate the whole proceeding, for the matter and form of the Sacraments, as Benedict XIV. teaches in his work, "De Synodo Diocesana" (l. viii., c. 10), belong to the substance of the Sacrament, and are declared by the Council of Trent to be unalterable (Sess. 21, c. 2). Such must be the judgment of theology, according to the principle of St. Thomas Aquinas :—"He who corrupts the sacramental words in uttering them, if he does this on purpose, does not appear to intend that which the Church does, and thus the Sacrament does not appear to be perfected" (P. 3, q. lx., a. 7, ad. 3). It must be borne in mind that St. Thomas, in writing his Summa, does not profess to do more than furnish a summary, for the use of students, of those principles of theology which had been handed down to his times by the unbroken tradition of what some are pleased to call the undivided Church.

It may, then, be accepted as proved :—

1. That in the Ordinal of Edward VI., those parts which had, up to that time, been held to constitute the sacramental forms, indispensable to the validity of the Sacrament, by which—and, up to the 14th century, by which alone—Orders were conferred, were omitted bodily.

2. That these alterations were made to give expression in the rite to the view that Orders were not a visible sign or ceremony ordained of God, had not the nature of a Sacrament, and bestowed no grace. (Compare Art. 25 with the definition of a Sacrament in the Catechism given previously.)

"Dr. Champneys and all Catholics," says Clerophilus Alethes,[1] "have ever attacked their Orders from the defect of that form." It may be well, therefore, to produce some evidence of the fact, and to see what

---

[1] Page 237.

effect this denial had upon both Catholics and Protestants in their dealings with Anglican Orders. For
this purpose it will be necessary to enter, at some
length, upon the history of the period. The light
which it throws upon the subject will reward us for
our labour.

Very soon after the alleged consecration of Parker,
the Catholic party openly challenged the valid ordination of those of the new learning, and called upon them
to produce, if they could, evidence of the fact.

The following are a few specimens of their line of
argument :—

1.   Harding fastens upon Jewel, and takes him to
task in this wise :—" Ye have abandoned the external
Sacrifice and Priesthood of the New Testament, and
have not in your sect consecrated Bishops, and therefore, being without priests made with lawful laying on
of hands, as Scripture requireth, all Orders being given
by Bishops only, how can you say that any among
you can lawfully minister, or that you have any lawful
minister at all ?"

He compares Jewel to Ischyras, who was no lawful
minister, as he was not lawfully ordained, because
Collythus, who pretended to ordain him, " died in
the degree of priesthood himself, and was never consecrated Bishop " (Harding's " Conference of Jewel,"
p. 58).   •

He concludes his argument as follows :—" Thus
they be neither priests nor deacons which be not
lawfully consecrated according to the order that is
used in the Church, that is, to wit, by Bishops lawfully consecrated, but either by the people as the lay
magistrate . . . . . or by monks and friars apostate,
or by excommunicated priests having no bishoply
power."

Again, he pursues Jewel in these words :—" You,
Jewel, bear yourself as though you were Bishop of
Salisbury. But how can you prove your vocation ?
By what authority usurp you the administration of

doctrine and the Sacraments? What can you allege
for the right and proof of your ministry? Who hath
called you? Who hath laid hands on you? By what
example hath he done it? How and by whom are
you consecrated? Who hath sent you? Who hath
committed to you the office you take upon you? Be
you a priest or be you not? If you be not, how dare
you usurp the name and office of a Bishop? If you
be, tell us who gave you orders? The institution of a
priest was never yet but in power of a Bishop. . . . . .
Show us the letter of your Orders. At least show us
that you have received powers to the office you presume to exercise, by due order of laying on of hands
and consecration. But order and consecration you
have not. . . . . . Though the Prince has thus promoted you, yet ye be presumers and thrusters in of
yourselves. Well, lands and manors the Prince may
give you; Priesthood and Bishopric the Prince cannot
give you."

Dr. Stapleton also follows Harding's line of argument, thus:—"Now the *pretended* Bishops of Protes-
tantism—whereas the whole number of our learned
and reverend pastors, for confession of the truth, were
displaced of their rooms, none being left in the realm
having authority to consecrate Bishops or make priests,
that being the office of only Bishops—by what authority do they govern the fold of Christ's flock? Who
laid hands upon them? . . . . . Whither went they to
be consecrated—into France, Spain, or Germany—
seeing that at home there was no number of such as
might and would serve their turn? . . . . . I say,
therefore, by the verdict of Holy Scripture and
practice of the primitive Church, these men are no
Bishops. I speak nothing of the laws of the realm;
it hath been of late sufficiently proved they are no
Bishops, if they be tried thereby. But let them be
tried by Scripture. . . . . . Your pretended Bishops
have no such ordination as the ancient Bishops had,
no such laying on of hands of other Bishops, no

authority to make true priests or ministers, and, therefore, neither are ye true ministers, neither are they any Bishops at all" ("Fortress of the Faith," p. 36).

The same writer, when dealing with Jewel's "Un-truths," says, that these men had "rushed into the ministry without any imposition of hands, and without any eccesiastical authority;" and at page 93, that they "began from themselves, receiving imposition of hands from nobody."

This writer's "Return of Untruths," his challenge to Jewel and Horn, and his Counterblast against them, are worth your perusal.

Bristow wrote some nine years later than Harding or Stapleton. He was Professor of Theology both at Douay and at Rheims, and deals with the question as a professed theologian. He calls the new ministers "laymen unsent, uncalled, unconsecrated" ("Motives," p. 91, 1574). "The King of England," he says, "and the Queen too, give their diplomas to whom they choose. Then these carry themselves as Bishops, and begin to ordain ministers."

"We have," he says again, "many examples in England — to wit, in the case of Parker, Grindal, Saunders, Horne, and others — who, having been ordained priests according to the Catholic rite, were judged fit to be, without any ordination, not only priests, but also Bishops, Archbishops, and Primates, either, by virtue of royal letters, or by a ridiculous consecration by those who had received the power of consecrating only from the Queen" (pp. 264–266).

This repeated assertion that Anglican Orders had no higher sanction in their origin than the royal authority, tends much to strengthen the suspicion that Barlow was Bishop only by royal "election;" a title which, we have seen, he held to be both sufficient and legitimate. For it would have been ruin to their cause if these writers grounded their charge on statements of fact which they did not know to be true, and which the parties most concerned could easily prove to be false.

It was quite notorious that the Pope and the Catholic Bishops regarded the innovators as *laymen*, as the following facts prove :—

1. Gardiner, in his sermon before the Legate on the first Sunday in Advent, thus describes them :— "But what kind of a head in fine was that of a Church, from which half the clergy were at once removed, and, the Priesthood being done away with, men, who were *laymen*, profane and married, were appointed as ministers, and in which, after a few years of that half, no clergy at all would have been left?" (Copy in Grenville Library).

2. Proceedings were instituted at Rome before Cardinal Riario to ascertain the real state of affairs in England. Twelve articles were proved by twelve witnesses at least, of which the seventh was :— " Whether by her (the Queen's) authority any schismatics, *who were not Priests*, had been appointed Bishops and rectors." Pius V., in the sentence pronounced in consequence, condemns her because, " by her own authority," she conferred " bishoprics, benefices, and other dignities upon schismatics, heretics, married men, and *persons who were not clerics*" (Continuation of Baronius' Annals by Laderchius, vol. iii., p. 197, 210).

Bullingham, who held the See of Lincoln, is specially named as one who was known to be a layman. Goldwell, Bishop of St. Asaph's, and the last of the English Bishops, was one of the witnesses.

3. The faculties granted by the Pope to the Bishops for reconciling the clergy limits their authority to recognising them in their Orders and retaining them in their benefices—only in those cases where " The form and intention of the Church had been observed in their ordination." In the case of persons holding benefices, *without being in any Orders*, they may be promoted to all even the Sacred Orders and

the priesthood, if found to be worthy and fit, and may retain their benefices if in other respects canonically conferred (Regist. Exped., vol. i., p. 32). There only the Orders of those ordained by the old Catholic Ritual are acknowledged as being any Orders at all.

4. The Enchiridion of Faith, by Francis Coventry, 2nd ed., Douay, 1655, in answer to the question, " *Whether ordination and jurisdiction are extinct in Protestants according to faith*," says, "This hath been always ventilated even from the beginning of the schism, and of late renewed in the case of Dr. Goffe, at Paris, *who was re-ordained, as all others have been*," &c.

On the death of Edward VI., and the accession of his sister Mary, the *status* of the newly-ordained clergy was a question that received her immediate attention. The claim to possess valid orders was a pretence of such notoriety that she deals with it as a fact beyond dispute, on which it was not necessary to wait for the Church to adjudicate. In her letter to Bonner, Art. 15, she directs :—" Item, touching such persons as were heretofore promoted to any orders, after the new sort and fashion of orders, considering they were not ordered in very deed, the Bishop of the diocese, finding otherwise sufficiency and ability in these men, may supply that thing which wanted in them before, and then, according to his discretion, admit them to minister."

Now, the thing that was wanting in them was that they were not "ordered in very deed."

The Bishops, made after the new sort and fashion of Orders, were deprived of their Sees for various reasons. The Commissions for proceeding against them are dated in March, 1553-4, and are given in Rymer (xv., 70). Taylor, of Lincoln, was deprived expressly " on account of the *nullity* of his consecration and defect in his title, which he held from King Edward VI. by letter-patent, with this clause : ' during his good behaviour' " ("Canterbury Register," March

20). Hooper, who had been consecrated by the Revised Ritual, was deprived on the same day for the same reason. Ferrar, of whom Collier says that his consecration " had not been altogether performed after the old form,"[1] was also deprived on the same day for the same reason. Harley was deprived with him, on the same grounds. Bird and Holgate, for their marriage. Bush resigned. Scory had to give up Chichester to the lawful Bishop, Day, and on his repentance was allowed to act as priest. It is also a fact worthy of being remembered, that when some of these " pretended " Bishops were degraded, before they were handed over to the secular power they were treated simply as priests, and degraded only from the priesthood, no notice being taken of their consecrations according to the Revised Ritual. Ferrar and Hooper were dealt with in this way.

Some attempt has been made to make capital out of the so-called rehabilitation of Scory by Bonner. The facts, however, tell quite the other way. There is not a particle of evidence that his episcopal character was ever recognised. Bonner did not refuse him out of courtesy the title of Bishop, which had been legally his ; but that was all. A Bishop has no power to deal with the case of a brother Bishop unless he is specially delegated by the higher Ecclesiastical authorities, to do so. And Bonner had not only received no such commission but in the faculties given him for reconciling the clergy — the case of Bishops is expressly reserved to the Legate ; so that the fact that Bonner dealt with Scory's case proves that he was recognised only as a priest, and that his episcopal character was quite ignored. Burnet bluntly says that the certificate given by Bonner to Scory was simply to the effect that he had put away the woman with whom he had been living, and was in a position to be restored to the exercise of his priesthood. The letter merely allows Scory to say mass in Bonner's diocese.

---

[1] Part II., book iv., No. 266.

When Pole landed in England, in the following November, there were, therefore, no Bishops, after the new sort and fashion of Orders, in the possession of any See, left for him to deal with. It is sufficiently probable that the English authorities were in communication with the Pope, and acted with his knowledge and sanction. The fact that their acts were not in any way questioned or appealed against, on the arrival of Pole, seems to point to that conclusion. However, what was done was confirmed.

The work of the Legate in England lay chiefly amongst the lower order of clergy. Some of them had been validly ordained according to the Roman Ritual, under Henry VIII., others had been ordained with cuts and omissions to suit the fancy of the Reformers. Others had been ordained in accordance with the new Ritual, and some not at all. In addition to this, heresy, schism, simony, and incontinence had brought upon some or other of them nearly every censure and punishment known to the canon law. It was, therefore, necessary that every case should be judged on its own merits, and that Cardinal Pole should not only have very large powers himself, but be able to delegate these powers to others, as it was quite impossible for one man to deal with every case likely to arise in consequence of the late state of affairs. Accordingly, Cardinal Pole received from Pope Julius III. a Bull, dated March 8, 1554, authorizing him to subdelegate to others the very large legatine faculties he had already received.

The perusal of this document is very instructive, as it shows how thoroughly the situation was understood at Rome. Speaking of those clergy who by reason of their crimes had incurred the censure of irregularity, he says that on repentance they may be absolved and allowed to exercise their Orders—" provided," however, " that before their fall into this heresy they had been rightly and lawfully promoted or ordained."

This clause excludes those who had been ordained by the Edwardine forms, for they had been ordained and promoted in direct violation of the canon law, and therefore unlawfully. We shall find later on that the evil thing about their ordination and appointment was, that it was not done according to the form and intention of the Church.

Another passage deals more directly with the question before us, as it separates off the ecclesiastics in England by the condition of the Orders they laid claim to.

The Pope empowers the Legate " Freely to use all and each of the aforesaid . . . . . faculties . . . . . in person, or through others appointed by thee for this purpose *pro tem.*, even as regards Orders which they had never or evilly received, and the rite of Consecration which was applied to them by other Bishops or Archbishops, even heretics or schismatics, or otherwise unduly and without following the accustomed form of the Church."

Here we have mention of three classes of persons to be dealt with : (1), Those who had not received Orders ; (2), Those who had received them evilly : (3), Those who had received them unduly.

Under which of these classes, then, are the Edwardine clerics to be ranked ? We have seen that Queen Mary, acting certainly under advice, ranks them in the first category by the words :- "Seeing they are not ordered in very deed." As do also the Bishops, who deprived Taylor, with other Edwardine prelates, expressly on the ground of the " nullity of his consecration."

Now, is there any reason to suppose that Cardinal Pole differed from the Queen and the Catholic Bishops in his estimate of the Revised Ordinal ? Quite the contrary. Not only did he allow their decision to hold good, but also, in the Commission granted to the Dean and Chapter of Canterbury for reconciling the clergy and laity of that Province, he expresses this agreement.

" The instrument," says Collier, " extends to the absolving of all persons who repent their miscarriages, and desire to be restored from all heresies, schisms, apostasies, from all excommunications, suspensions, and other Ecclesiastical censures ; and more particularly the clergy who had received Orders from any schismatical or heretical Bishops, officiated in virtue of that character, and complied with any unallowed ceremonies and forms of prayer, are absolved, *provided the Form and Intention of the Church was not omitted in their ordination.*" [1]

I have shown already, beyond all question, that this was the very thing done in the Revised Ritual. Both the Form and the Intention of the Church were tampered with. Schismatical and heretical Orders are allowed to stand after repentance and absolution ; not so, however, in the case where the Form and Intention of the Church were omitted.

You will notice that the two points insisted on throughout these quotations are :—(1), Unlawfulness of title or promotion ; (2), Invalidity of Orders, in the case of those promoted after the new sort and fashion of Orders.

On the death of Queen Mary, her sister, Queen Elizabeth, set herself to undo the work of the last reign, and to introduce again the new religion, and, along with it, the Revised Ordinal. The difficulties in her way were serious. None of the Bishops of the English Hierarchy would have anything to do with her or her Ordinal. They were, therefore, deposed, with the exception of Kitchen, of Landaff. As they refused to hand on the succession to the Queen's nominees, and as they were the only persons who could lawfully do so, on the principle, " *Quod non habetis, non potestis dare*," the lawful succession in the Church of England would on their death become extinct. In this extremity, the Queen bethought

---

[1] Part II., book v., No. 377.

herself of her Royal Supremacy in spiritual matters
over the Church, and on her own authority commis-
sioned four of her creatures to consecrate Parker by
an instrument in which the following dispensation was
inserted, to cover all the irregularity and deficiency in
the proceeding :—" Supplying, nevertheless, by our
supreme Royal authority, of our mere motion and
certain knowledge, if anything either in those things
which shall be done by you according to our foresaid
mandate, or in you or any one of you, is or shall be
wanting in condition, *status*, or faculty, of those things
which are required or are necessary by the statutes of
this kingdom, or by Ecclesiastical laws in this matter,
the nature of the time and the necessity of the circumstances requiring it."

This clause is remarkable from the use of the
technical terms " of our mere motion and certain
knowledge," which are used in Papal documents to
indicate their unreserved application to all cases.

Those who confirmed Parker in his dignity quote
this clause in their commission as the authority for
their acts. They say, " The election of the venerable
man, Mr. Mathew Parker, we confirm by the supreme
authority of the said most serene Lady, our Queen,
committed unto us in his behalf; supplying by the
supreme Royal authority, of the Queen's mere motion
and certain knowledge, delegated to us, all defects in
this election, as well in those things done by us and
proceeded with according to the commandment given
us, or that are or shall be in ourselves or in the
condition, *status*, or capacity of any one of us for this
performance " (Bramhall, iii., 202). Nor is this all.

The validity of the consecration of Parker and also
the validity of the consecration of the Queen's Bishops,
as well as their lawful authority, were seriously questioned in many quarters, and doubts were freely
expressed on the subject. To set the whole matter
at rest, an Act was passed in 1565 (8 Eliz., c. 1.), to
decree " that all acts and things heretofore had, made,

or done by any person or persons in or about any
⎨ *consecration*, confirmation, or investing of any person
or persons elected to the office or dignity of any
Archbishop or Bishop within this realm, or within any
other the Queen's Majesty's dominions or countries,
by virtue of the Queen's Majesty's letter patent or
commission since the beginning of her Majesty's reign,
be and shall be *by the authority of this present Parliament* declared, judged, and deemed, at and from every
of the several times of the doing thereof, good and
perfect to all respects and purposes ; *any matter or
thing that can or may be objected to the contrary
thereof in any wise notwithstanding.*"

If it be within the scope of the civil power to make
good and perfect consecrations in Holy Orders by the
authority of Parliament — anything to the contrary
notwithstanding—then those of the Queen's Bishops
are, beyond question, valid. You, however, agree
with me so far, that the Apostolic succession and
valid Orders must have a higher sanction than even
the weighty authority of the British Parliament.

The Catholics were not the only persons who
pronounced the Revised Ordinal worthless. The
Scotch Presbyterians, on the very same grounds,
argued that there were no Bishops in the Establishment ; that, in fact, it was Presbyterian because
the Ordinal was insufficient to make a Bishop. So
straight did they drive their argument home, that
in order to meet it the Consecration Service was
altered to its present form — a hundred years and
more too late to be of any use to the line of prelates
which it introduced.

Burnet, in his " History of the Reformation," [1]
speaks of this alteration as follows :—" They agreed
on a form of ordaining deacons, priests, and Bishops,
which is the same we yet (*i.e.*, A.D. 1683) use, except
in some few words that have been added since in the

---

[1] Part II., book i., page 144, ed. 1683.

ordination of a priest or Bishop. For there was then no express mention made, in the words of ordaining them, that it was for the one or the other office. In both it was said, ' Receive thou the Holy Ghost, in the name of the Father,' &c. . . . . . But that having been since made use of to prove both functions the same, it was of late years altered as it is now."

Such then, in short, are the considerations which ought to guide an inquirer as to the validity of Anglican Orders, and which seem to me sufficient for all practical purposes, to close the question. I have confined my remarks, as you cannot fail to have noticed, chiefly to the consecration of Bishops, because, if there are no validly consecrated Bishops there can be no Orders of any kind in the Established Church.

I have maintained, from an historical point of view, the *unlawfulness* of attempting to exercise such Orders: (1), Because of the grave reasons there are for thinking that some at least of the Protestant Bishops were never formally even Christians, on account of their never having received any certainly valid Christian Baptism, and hence were incapable of receiving any valid Christian Orders. That there have been some such is beyond a doubt ; and the very loose theology and practice of former days on the subject of baptismal regeneration render it more than probable that there have been many others. (2), Because we know for certain that, till the Act of Uniformity was passed, a very large number of persons acting as clergy never even pretended to have received ordination to the priesthood from any Bishop. These grave doubts as to Baptism and Priesthood create a state of uncertainty as to the existence of Orders in any given case, in which it is not safe, and hence not *lawful*, to act.

I have further maintained the absolute *invalidity* of Anglican Orders because of the omission in the Revised Ritual, amongst other things, of the " Prayer of Consecration," which had, up to that time, been considered part of the essential sacramental Form of Holy Orders. An omission made without any authority, and one so serious, that you might almost as well hold that if the words, "I baptise thee in the name of the Father," &c., were omitted in baptism, the other passages in the Ritual would supply the deficiency.

The only answer that can be attempted to this is, to say that our Lord ordained His Apostles by the form, "Receive the Holy Ghost," and that the Holy See in the case of the Abyssinian ordinations has allowed the sufficiency of this Form.

But, in the first place, you know that theologians generally hold that Christ determined, substantially at least, the Matter and Form of all the Sacraments before His Ascension, and the fact that the words, "Receive the Holy Ghost," were not used in the West till about the 14th century, would seem to leave no question as to their not being the Sacramental Form; for, if so, this sacrament has been lost to the Church.

The power of the priesthood is twofold : one, sacramental, over the real Body of Christ in the Holy Eucharist. This power was given to the Apostles by the words : "*Do this in commemoration of Me.*" And hence the Council of Florence, in the Decree of Union, has laid down that "The Form of the priesthood is this :—'*Receive power to offer sacrifice for the living and the dead, in the name of the Father,*'" &c., which is substantially the same as the former. Without the bestowal of this power Orders are impossible. The other power of the priesthood is judicial *in foro interiore* over the mystical body of Christ. This is the power that is considered to be given by the words, "Receive the Holy Ghost," and can be given only to one who already is a priest. Our Lord Himself conferred them separately, as is evident; giving the former at the Last Supper, and the latter after the Resurrection. The *sine quâ non* of the priesthood, *i.e.*, power to consecrate, was not given on the latter occasion by the words then used.

As regards the decision of the Holy See in reference to Abyssinian Orders, you are probably by this time aware that Canon Estcourt, who put forth the opinion you allude to, laboured under a very serious misapprehension. He was quite wrong in supposing that therein the sufficiency of the words, " Receive the Holy Ghost," as a Sacramental Form, was established. Even if it were so for the priesthood, nothing would follow as regards the Episcopacy. However, I submit for your perusal the repudiation by the Holy See of any intention to decide the matter in this sense.

Letter of Cardinal Patrizi to his Eminence the Cardinal Archbishop of Westminster.

" To the Lord Cardinal, Archbishop of Westminster. —*April 30th, 1875.*

" Most Eminent and most Reverend Lord, — In your letter of the 24th of August of last year, your Eminence called attention to a question now discussed by several writers as to the meaning attaching to a certain 'decree,' as it is termed, issued by the Supreme Congregation of the Holy Inquisition on the 10th of April, 1704, in a certain Abyssinian case, regarding the validity of ordination conferred by the words, ' *Receive ye the Holy Ghost,*' joined with imposition of hands ; and (you mentioned) that it had given the Anglicans ground for asserting and boasting that in future Catholics could entertain no doubt of the validity of Anglican Orders. Wherefore, to remove all cause of anxiety and to defend the truth more securely, your Eminence requested a solution of the following doubt : namely, whether the doctrine that imposition of hands joined to these words only, ' *Receive ye the Holy Ghost,*' suffices for the validity of the Order of Priesthood, was contained implicitly or explicitly in the above-named decree.

" On Wednesday, the 24th of the present month, it was decided by the Most Eminent Fathers the

Cardinals, who share with me the office of Inquisitor General, after a mature discussion of the question, that an answer must be returned *in the negative*. And one or two of the motives which guided them in this decision will suffice to convince your Eminence of the justice of this Decree. For it is manifest from the Coptic rite, as given in their Pontifical books, that the words, ' *Receive ye the Holy Ghost,*' do not constitute the entire form ; nor is the meaning of the document, dating from 1704 (which document is not a Decree of the Sacred Congregation, as appears from its Archives), to be understood as implying more than this—that the ordination of a priest among the Copts, conferred by the laying on of hands and the pronouncing of the form prescribed by their ancient rite, is to be considered valid ; nor has the Holy Supreme Congregation ever declared, explicitly or implicitly, that the imposition of hands with no other words than ' *Receive ye the Holy Ghost*' suffices for the validity of the Order of Priesthood.

" With the consciousness of having complied with the duties of my office, it only remains for me to kiss, with all due reverence and humility, your Eminence's hand.

" Your Eminence's most humble and
          devoted servant,

"(Signed)   C. CARDINAL PATRIZI.

" Rome, *April 30th, 1875.*"

Some persons, who seem to forget that discretion is the better part of valour, may perhaps resent what I have written as an attack upon their honour and an insult to their Church. With such I do not care to dispute ; you know me too well to suppose for a moment that I have any such intention.

I have written solely with the view of bringing home to you what I believe to be the truth, and in the spirit of the most perfect charity. This is a question upon which the salvation of your soul may depend, and eternity is altogether too serious an issue to allow of your risking it at a game of *rouge et noir ;* for this is what you are doing now.

The whole Catholic Church never has accepted and never can accept Anglican Orders, and never ceases to cry aloud to those who would sustain the spirits of their followers by asserting that when they come over in a body she will make terms with them, " No illusions, gentlemen—no illusions !"

On the other hand, what have you to' fall back upon? Beyond the assurance of your leaders and your own private judgment—nothing. What guarantee have you that both they and you may not be mistaken ? None whatever.   Suppose you find, when it is too late, that you have made a mistake—what then ? The whole of the Catholic Church, the Schismatical , Greek Church, even the body you called your Mother Church, were witnesses to you that you were clinging to a phantom.   You would not have it so ; you staked your soul on the issue that you were right and all the world in the wrong—and you have lost.

Yours sincerely,

J. D. BREEN.